• Llangollen • Berwyn • Glyndyfrdwy • Carrog • Corwen •

LLANGOLLEN RAILWAY

Country Walks
From Our Stations
Peter Dickinson

© Peter Dickinson 2022

All rights reserved. No part of this publication may be reproduced, stored in a retrieval system or transmitted, in any form or by any means, electronic, mechanical, photocopying, recording or otherwise, without prior permission in writing from Silver Link Books, Mortons Media Group Ltd.

First published in 2022

British Library Cataloguing in Publication Data

A catalogue record for this book is available from the British Library.

ISBN 978 1 85794 571 3

Silver Link Books
Mortons Media Group Limited
Media Centre
Morton Way
Horncastle
LN9 6JR
Tel/Fax: 01507 529535

email: sohara@mortons.co.uk
Website: www.nostalgiacollection.com

Printed and bound in Turkey.

Please follow the Country Code

- Enjoy the countryside and respect its life and work
- Fasten all gates
- Leave property as you find it
- Keep to public paths across farmland
- Use gates and stiles to cross fences, hedges and walls
- Wear suitable clothing and shoes
- Take care when crossing and walking along country roads
- Take your litter home
- Guard against the risk of fire
- Keep your dogs under close control
- Protect wildlife, plants and trees
- Make no unnecessary noise
- Leave nothing but footprints, take nothing but pictures, kill nothing but time

Recommended maps:

- OS Explorer Map 255 – Llangollen & Berwyn
- OS Explorer Map 256 – Wrexham & Llangollen

Contents

Introduction
About the Llangollen Railway

WALK 1 – Old railway from Llangollen to Trevor
WALK 2 – Llangollen to Castell Dinas Brân
WALK 3 – Plas Newydd Circular Walk
WALK 4 – Llangollen to Berwyn
WALK 5 – Horseshoe Falls Circular Walk
WALK 6 – Llantysilio and Velvet Hill Circular Walk
WALK 7 – Glyndyfrdwy Circular
WALK 8 – Carrog to Glyndyfrdwy
WALK 9 – Corwen to Caer Drewyn Circular Walk
WALK 10 – Old railway Circular Walk from Corwen

Further reading

Introduction

Welcome to this new walking guidebook featuring 10 country walks from the Llangollen Railway's stations.

The idea of promoting walks from LR stations goes back to an A5-sized leaflet I produced back in 2013 to assist walkers visiting the iconic Horseshoe Falls from Berwyn station. I hope that you enjoy doing the walks as much as I have. They cover options from simple strolls to more challenging rambles, and all feature the varied and beautiful scenery that the Dee Valley has to offer.

Reasonable footwear is recommended as some parts can be muddy, and please bear in mind the times of the trains to take you back.

All the walks in this book were checked in the summer of 2019, but please note that land usage and fence lines can alter over time.

Peter Dickinson
Bromsgrove, Worcestershire

Key:
FP = Footpath
SP = Signpost

Front cover: LNWR 'Coal Tank' No 58926 pilots LNWR 'Super D' No 49395 out of Berwyn.
Clive Hanley

About The Llangollen Railway

Stepping on board one of the Llangollen Railway's trains is a ticket to your own personal railway adventure.

The Llangollen Railway, a true country line of the old Great Western Railway, was opened more than 150 years ago and offers a nostalgic ride back in time. The historic steam and diesel locomotives transport passengers from Llangollen, the riverside town where 'Wales welcomes the World', to the picturesque market town of Corwen.

Along the way the railway remains close to the tumbling waters of the River Dee, all set within an Area of Outstanding Natural Beauty (AONB). The gently rolling hills, unspoilt villages and farms nestling in leafy lanes, the beautiful Valle Crucis Abbey and an internationally important World Heritage Site are all waiting to be discovered.

The five unique stations linked by the 10-mile scenic journey offer the perfect starting points to further explore the Dee Valley and will repay hours of exploration. This Walking Guide will be the perfect companion for you to get the most of your visit to the Llangollen Railway and the wider Dee Valley. There are some gentle climbs but for the most part a pair of walking boots or sturdy shoes should get you through. Make sure you have the railway's timetable with you if want to catch a train to complete your day out.

The history of the Llangollen Railway is the story of a colossal struggle to keep a dying part of Britain's heritage alive, a struggle that still goes on today. The railway was once part of a cross-country route linking the railway junction of Ruabon in the east with the seaside resort of Barmouth in the west. The route developed into an important artery across rural Wales, bringing in its wake a revolution in agriculture, industry and daily life. Seasonal holiday traffic became big business, tapping into the expanding conurbations of Liverpool, Manchester and Birmingham.

However, the influx of cars, lorries and buses on Britain's roads soon made the railway a liability rather than a vital service in the eyes of the Government, and after a century of service the line was closed. The railway tracks were lifted and the surviving infrastructure began to decay. This is where the battle to preserve the Llangollen Railway began.

Starting in 1975, a small band of enthusiasts set about restoring and rebuilding a section of the railway from the derelict Llangollen station, setting their sights on the next town of Corwen. Despite facing many challenges and obstacles, heritage trains returned to the valley and once again link the two towns.

The story does not end there. The Llangollen Railway continues to develop its services and expand, and with the invaluable help of its staff and volunteers will hopefully continue to do so for many years to come.

Route Map of The Llangollen Railway

LLANGOLLEN

Walk 1

WALK 1 – Old railway from Llangollen to Trevor

Distance: 4.5 miles (7.25km) or 9 miles (14.5km) circular walk

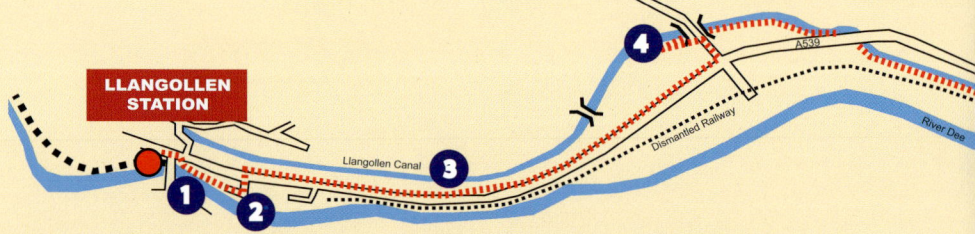

This walk follows the route of the old railway line eastwards from Llangollen, including sections along the former trackbed.

On leaving Llangollen station, cross over Castle Road at the end of the river bridge. At the traffic lights adjacent to the Bridge End Hotel, take the steps down on the right **(1)**. This riverside FP follows the trackbed of the old railway as far as the

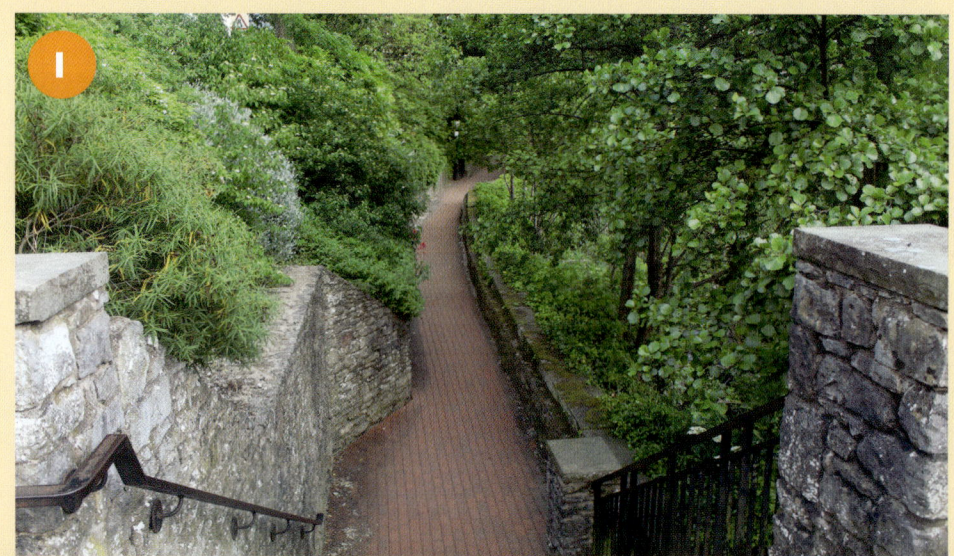

Walk 1 Old railway from Llangollen to Trevor

Long Stay car park behind the Ponsonby Arms public house. Turn right at the car park exit and follow the main road towards the Health Centre, crossing over the road when possible **(2)**.

Beyond the Health Centre, the old trackbed becomes visible alongside the main road and hosts the metallic Hawthorn sculpture erected in 2004.

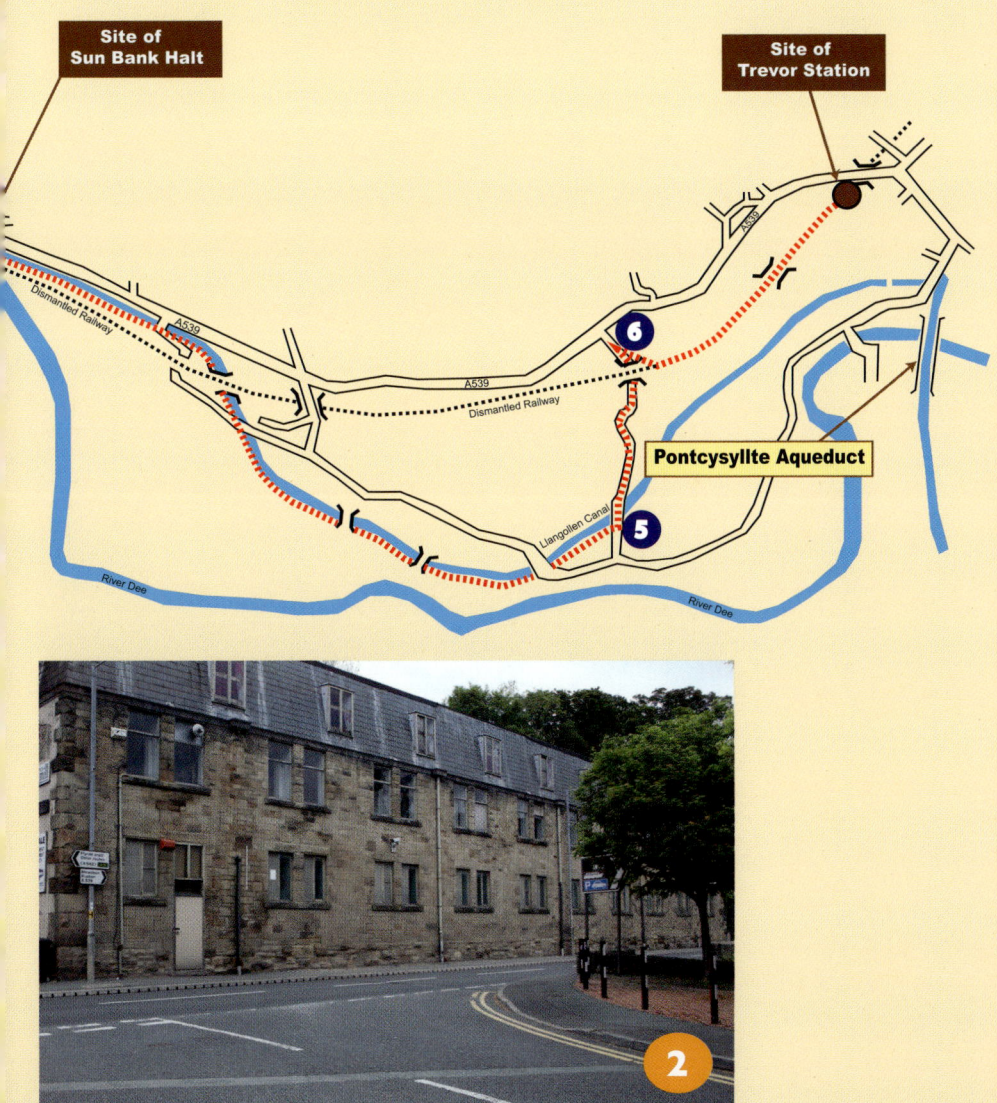

Follow the main road **(3)** before turning left at the next lane signed 'Llanddyn'. This will take you up to the Llangollen Canal. Join the canal towpath at bridge 43W **(4)** and follow it for 2 miles downstream, passing under the main road at bridge 42W.

Beyond the bridge, the trackbed of

Walk 1 Old railway from Llangollen to Trevor

the railway comes into view below the towpath to your right. The minor road that passes over the canal at Bridge 41W **(5)** originally gave access to the railway's Sun Bank Halt, although few traces of the station survive today. Bridge 39W marks the point where the railway passed over the canal; the bridge itself remains in remarkable condition despite not having had a train on it for more than 50 years! Beyond the bridge, the Bryn Howel Hotel can be seen, which was built in the late 1800s by a Mr Edwards who owned quarries and brick and tile works locally.

Leave the towpath immediately after Bridge 34W, bearing right and carefully following the lane over the bridge for one-third of a mile. Proceed until the former 'Plasynpentre' railway bridge comes into view, then follow the 'Old Railway Line' pathway up on your right **(6)**. This follows the route of the former railway as far as the

old Trevor railway station, where the platform edges can still be seen within the woodland.

Once at the old station site, it is possible to either retrace your steps the 4.5 miles back to Llangollen station, or catch one of the regular No 5 or T3 buses from the bus stop on the main road (A539).

Walk 2 — LLANGOLLEN — LLANGOLLEN RAILWAY

WALK 2 – Llangollen to Castell Dinas Brân

Distance: 2 miles (3.25km)

On leaving Llangollen station, cross over the road to the Bridge End Hotel and Riverside Taxidermy Studio. Turn left and climb up Wharf Hill. After crossing the canal, follow the path straight on at the T-junction (SP for Castell Dinas Brân) **(1)**.

Walk 2 Llangollen to Castel Dinas Brân

Follow the path as it ascends, keeping the High School on your left, **(2)** and pass through a kissing gate **(3)**. Cross the lane and continue up the hill (signposted 'To The Castle'). Pass through another kissing gate **(4)** adjacent to Pear Tree Cottage

THE LLANGOLLEN RAILWAY

and continue along the lane through the woods.

At the crossroads, continue straight on (SP for Castell Dinas Brân) until a metal kissing gate is reached. A small metal crow can be found perched on top of the gatepost here **(5)** – 'Dinas Brân' almost certainly means 'the Crow's Fortress'.

Take the right-hand path upwards to

Walk 2 Llangollen to Castel Dinas Brân

reach a plateau with a spectacular view of Castell Dinas Brân. This seemingly impregnable stronghold was built in the 1260s by the local Welsh ruler, Prince Gruffudd ap Madoc, on the site of a prehistoric hill fort. The castle was destined to have a very short active life, being burned by its Welsh defenders in 1277 in the face of a threatened English attack. It was then briefly held by English forces, before finally being abandoned soon after 1282.

To reach the ruins of Dinas Brân, follow the zigzag path up the southern flank of the hillside **(6)**. The dramatic placement of the ruins high above the Dee valley offers unrivalled views down on the town of Llangollen. In more recent centuries, famous painters like Turner and Wilson have captured the essence of Castell Dinas Brân on canvas.

To return to Llangollen's railway station, simply retrace your steps back down the hillside (SP Llangollen).

LLANGOLLEN

LLANGOLLEN RAILWAY

WALK 3 – Plas Newydd Circular Walk

Distance: 1.5 miles (2.5 km)

At the top of the exit ramp from Llangollen Station, turn right and cross the Llangollen Bridge over the railway and River Dee **(1)**. Turn right into Dee Lane at the southern end of the bridge, then turn right at the fork outside The Corn Mill

to join the Victoria Promenade. This riverside walkway was opened in 1897 to commemorate the Diamond Jubilee of Queen Victoria.

Take the first footpath up on your left and continue along Parade Street, passing the Llangollen Museum on your left **(2)**.

Opposite the town's War Memorials, turn right and proceed along Castle Street. At the traffic lights, carefully cross the A5 road before turning left (SP Oswestry & Shrewsbury). Turn right and ascend Hill Street (SP Plas Newydd ¼ mile) **(3)**, taking care as the footpath merges into

THE LLANGOLLEN RAILWAY

the roadway in places.

Turn left and enter the grounds of Plas Newydd house **(4)**. This was the home of two Irish ladies, Lady Eleanor Butler and Miss Sarah Ponsonby, during the late 1700s, who became known as the 'Ladies of Llangollen'. They received a stream of visitors to their little cottage, which over the years they transformed into a Gothic fantasy of projecting stained glass and elaborately carved oak. Plas Newydd is now in the ownership of Denbighshire County Council, with an exhibition inside the house featuring some of the ladies' possessions and an audio tour bringing their story back to life.

Outside the tearoom and shop, turn right and follow the footpath along the

Walk 3 Plas Newydd Circular Walk

edge of the bowling green **(5)**, before descending into the wooded glen. Three attractive stone bridges **(6)** and the ladies' restored summerhouse are passed on your right, before following the footpath upwards towards Plas Newydd house. At the decorative black and white Water Tower, turn right towards the house. Turn left in front of Plas Newydd house **(7)** and proceed back through the tranquil

gardens to the main entrance.

Turn immediately right and follow Butler's Hill as it descends towards the A5 road **(8)**. Worthy of note on the right-hand side is the Grade 2 listed Capel Pont Felin Hen, which was built in 1773 by members of a small congregation and was the first Methodist chapel in Llangollen.

Carefully cross the A5 road and proceed along Church Street and Bridge

Street. No 18 on the left-hand side of Church Street is the last sub-medieval externally timber-framed house in Llangollen and dates from the early 1600s **(9)**. At the end of Bridge Street is Centenary Square, which hosts the town's War Memorials and was completed in 2018 to mark the 100th anniversary of the end of the Great War **(10)**. Turn right into Castle Street and proceed back over Llangollen Bridge to the railway station.

LLANGOLLEN

WALK 4 – Llangollen to Berwyn

Distance: 1.75 miles (3 km)

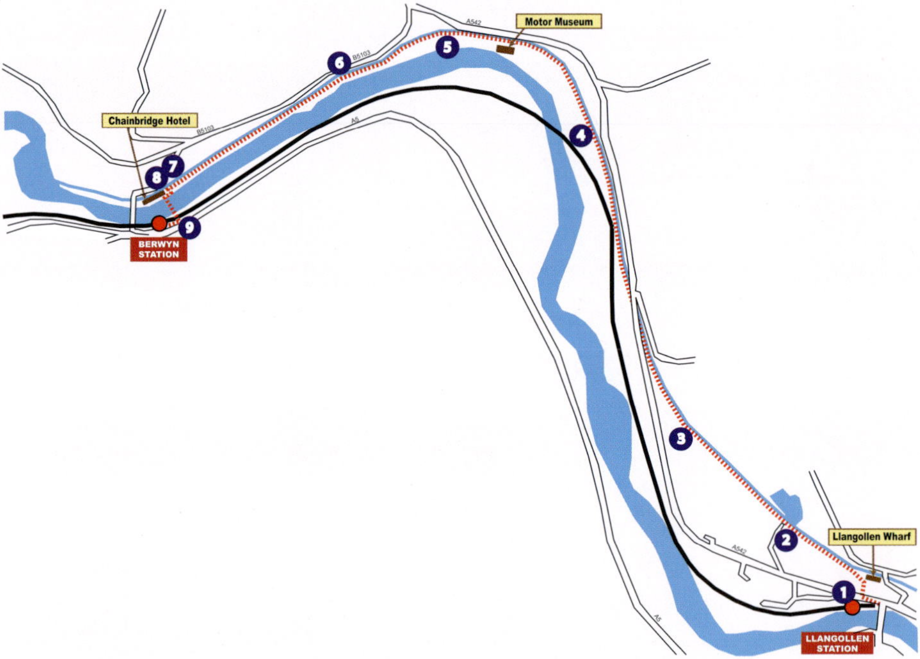

On leaving Llangollen station, turn left and cross the A542 Abbey Road towards the red post-box. Turn left and continue a few paces until reaching the Cwrt Glan y Gamlas Retirement Living complex. Turn right and follow the footpath (Brown SP for Canal) up to the Llangollen Wharf and canal **(1)**.

The Llangollen Wharf pleasure boat company was founded back in 1884 and visitors can still enjoy one of the horse-drawn boat trips that depart from the Wharf today.

Follow the canal towpath westwards (upstream), passing the canal boat moorings of Llangollen Basin on your right **(2)**. This marks the limit of navigation for motorised canal boats; only the horse-

Walk 4 Llangollen to Berwyn

21

THE LLANGOLLEN RAILWAY

drawn boat trips can proceed beyond this point.

On your left, the large pavilion is the home of the Llangollen International Musical Eisteddfod, which takes place every year during the second week of July. Famous performers here over the years have included Luciano Pavarotti, Katherine Jenkins, Lulu, Alfie Boe, Barbara Dickson and Bryn Terfel.

The canal towpath offers a tranquil route out of Llangollen as it winds its

Walk 4 Llangollen to Berwyn

5

way past cottages **(3)** and through trees towards Berwyn **(4-6)**. Just after the mid-point of this walk, the Llangollen Motor Museum is passed on the left and offers a fascinating trip down 'memory lane'. The museum sports more than 60 vehicles from cars to invalid carriages, including an Isetta bubble car, a Model T Ford, a Sinclair C5 and even pedal cars.

Upon reaching the Chainbridge Hotel,

6

THE LLANGOLLEN RAILWAY

pass through the wooden arbour (SP The Chainbridge Hotel Entrance) **(7)** and head through the covered walkway until reaching the chain bridge itself **(8)**. Cross the River Dee and follow the path as it zigzags up to the eastern end of Berwyn station **(9)**.

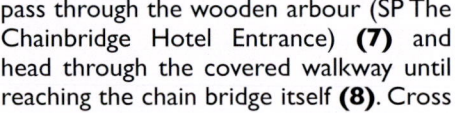

Walk 5

BERWYN

LLANGOLLEN RAILWAY

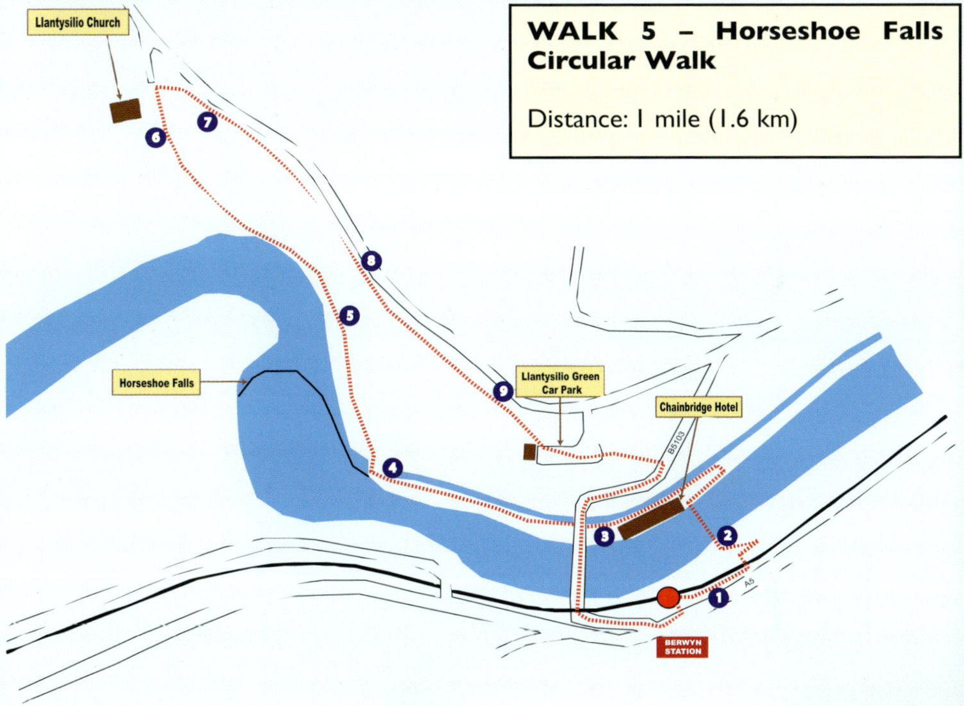

WALK 5 – Horseshoe Falls Circular Walk

Distance: 1 mile (1.6 km)

At the eastern (Llangollen) end of Berwyn station, follow the footpath down and pass under the railway line **(1)**. Close inspection of the white-glazed bricks on the walls of the bridge will reveal poignant pencil messages left by soldiers during the First World War, including one that simply states, 'I really want this baby'.

Continue along the footpath and cross the river

by the chain bridge **(2)**. There has been a river crossing here since the early 1800s and the bridge is now reputedly the oldest chain link bridge in the world.

At the northern end of the chain bridge, bear right and head through the covered walkway in front of the Chainbridge Hotel. At the canal, turn left and follow the towpath upstream behind the hotel.

Beyond Bridge 49AW (known as the King's Bridge as it was built to commemorate King Edward VII) **(3)**, the canal passes through woodland before

Walk 5 Horseshoe Falls Circular Walk

(4)

reaching the Meter House and Horseshoe Falls.

The Horseshoe Falls **(4)** were designed by Thomas Telford to supply water to the Llangollen Canal and were completed in 1808. Today around 12 million gallons of water are drawn in here each day from the River Dee, providing a water supply to the canal and helping to supply south Cheshire with drinking water.

Follow the path onwards (SP Llantysilio Church) **(5)**, passing through a kissing gate,

then a metal gate. St Tysilio's church on the left **(6)** was probably built in the 1400s, although there is evidence of earlier carved stonework around the small north window. Buried in the graveyard is German-born Charles Frederick Beyer, co-founder in 1853 of the Beyer Peacock steam locomotive factory in Manchester.

At the church's lych-gate, bear right following the way markers for the

Walk 5 Horseshoe Falls Circular Walk

Llangollen History Trail **(7)**. This section provides a panoramic view overlooking the Horseshoe Falls **(8)**, ending next to the public toilet block in the Llantysilio Green car park **(9)**.

At the end of the car park, follow the wooded path down to the B5103 lane, then bear right to cross the River Dee by the King's Bridge back to Berwyn station.

BERWYN

Walk 6

LLANGOLLEN RAILWAY

WALK 6 – Llantysilio and Velvet Hill Circular Walk

Distance: 4 miles (6.5km)

Note: At the time of writing (June 2019) the section of footpath across the fields between the Britannia Inn and Velvet Hill was found to be blocked by an electric fence at its southern end. It is up to the walker's discretion whether to take a detour or not.

At the eastern (Llangollen) end of Berwyn station, follow the footpath down and pass under the railway line (**1**). Close inspection of the white-glazed bricks on the walls of the bridge will reveal poignant pencil messages left by soldiers during the First World War, including one that simply states, 'I really want this baby'.

Continue along the footpath and cross the river by the chain bridge. There has been a river crossing here since the early 1800s and the bridge is now reputedly the oldest chain link bridge in the world.

At the northern end of the chain bridge, bear

Walk 6 Llantysilio and Velvet Hill Circular Walk

right and head through the covered walkway in front of the Chainbridge Hotel. At the canal, turn left and follow the towpath upstream behind the hotel **(2)**.

Beyond Bridge 49AW (known as the King's Bridge as it was built to commemorate King Edward VII), the canal passes through woodland before reaching the Meter House and Horseshoe Falls **(3)**. Follow the path onwards (SP Llantysilio

Church), passing through a kissing gate then a metal gate.

At the church's lych-gate **(4)**, bear left onto the road, following the way markers for the Dee Valley Way. Continue past the entrance of Llantysilio Hall and Llantysilio

Farm until a road junction is reached. Go through the wooden stile in the hedgerow a few paces beyond the red post-box **(5)**.

Climb along a rutted track, which keeps the woodland to your left and climbs northwards on a high pastured hillside **(6)**. Beyond the wooden stile **(7)**, turn right and continue to ascend, keeping parallel with the top edge

WALK 6 LLANTYSILIO AND VELVET HILL CIRCULAR WALK

of another wood. Take the right-hand fork in the path at the next two junctions as it skirts along the hillside **(8-9)**.

The path then descends to a complex of cottages at Pen-y-bryn. Pass through the stile and the narrow ginnel to the right of the first cottage. Follow the driveway down to the A542 Horseshoe Pass road at the Britannia Inn **(10)**.

Turn right and carefully follow the A542, before turning right when you get to the first junction. Use the first stile on your left (green FP sign) to head south across three fields **(11)**. Turn right along the farm track, then turn left past the

Hendy Isa holiday cottage to arrive at a narrow lane. Continue along the lane, keeping the Abbey Grange Hotel and campsite on your left until reaching the A542 Horseshoe Pass road again.

There is a choice of ways here. If you wish to climb Velvet Hill (the view from the top is magnificent!), go over the stile on the right (SP Velvet Hill) **(12)** and ascend beside the quarry workings. Upon reaching a wide grassy track, turn right and ascend through the bracken to reach the ridge **(13-14)**. Turn left to reach the summit of Velvet Hill, then descend on a narrow footpath into the woods. At the first stile, turn right and descend to the B5103 road junction alongside Bryntysilio Outdoor Education Centre. Follow

Walk 6 Llantysilio and Velvet Hill Circular Walk

the B5103 (SP Corwen 8 miles) over the King's Bridge to reach Berwyn station.

Alternatively, if you wish to avoid the climb to the summit of Velvet Hill, follow the footpath alongside the A542 Horseshoe Pass road. On the left is the Cistercian monastery of Valle Crucis Abbey, now under the care of Cadw and well worth a visit. Just beyond the Abbey Dingle Care Home, go over the stile on the right and follow the path up through the bracken and around the side of Velvet Hill. Ignore the first path that branches off to your left, but at the second junction cross the stile on your left and descend to the B5103 road junction alongside Bryntysilio Outdoor Education Centre. Follow the B5103 (SP Corwen 8 miles) **(15)** over the King's Bridge to reach Berwyn station.

Walk 7 — GLYNDYFRDWY

LLANGOLLEN RAILWAY

WALK 7 – Glyndyfrdwy Circular

Distance: 1.25 miles (2km)

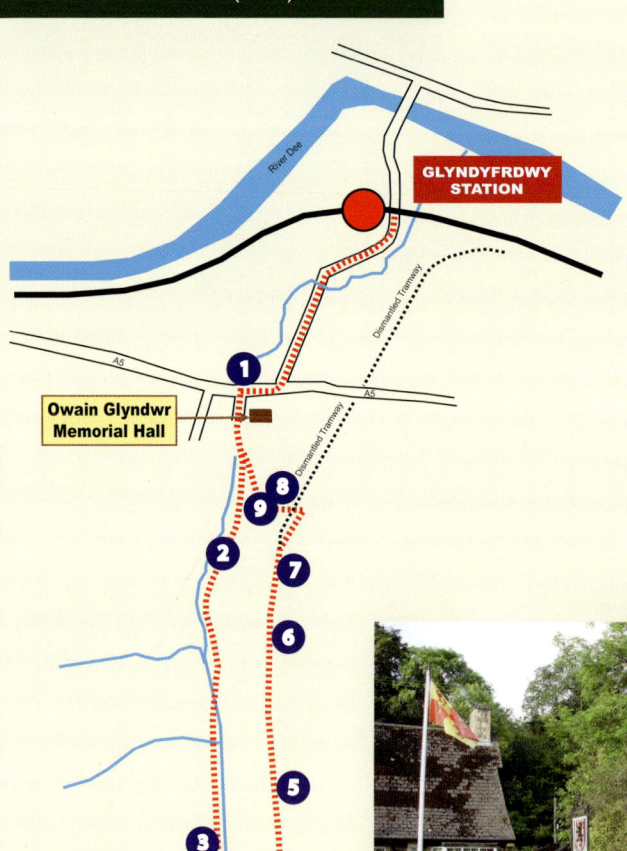

At the level crossing end of Glyndyfrdwy station, turn right and follow the lane up the hill. At the T-junction with the main A5 road, turn right and proceed for a few paces (SP North Berwyn Way). Carefully cross the A5 road in front of the Owain Glyndwr Memorial Hall **(I)**. This hall was built with funds raised by the community on the site of a woollen mill and was officially opened by the Prince of Wales in 1934.

Follow the track along the side of the hall (SP Nant-y-Pandy) and proceed through a wooden gate. Proceed straight on along the track, ignoring the footpath that rises steeply on your left

Walk 7 Glyndyfrdwy Circular

(we will use this footpath on our return) **(2)**. Follow the track as it crosses a bridge over the stream near Pandy Cottage **(3)**. Proceed on as the path gently climbs for another quarter-mile. Here a broad level area within the woods marks the site of

The Llangollen Railway

the former Pandy Mill **(4)**.

The mill was powered by a 30-foot-diameter water wheel, which operated a series of slate sawing and planing machines. By the mid-1800s a mile-long woodenway had been built to bring rough slabs of slate down from the nearby quarries, terminating at the mill.

With the arrival of the railway at Glyndyfrdwy station in 1865, the quarrying operations were greatly expanded. A new tramway down to the railway was built in 1876, serving the quarries until the 1940s. Our route will now encompass the former trackbed of the tramway back towards Glyndyfrdwy.

At the start of the widened Pandy

Mill area **(4)** within the woods, turn left and follow the footpath over the stream and along the valley side **(5)**. Remnants of the tramway's wooden sleepers can still be found embedded along this path. Proceed

Walk 7 Glyndyfrdwy Circular

over the stile alongside a wooden gate. Beyond the slate retaining wall on the right **(6)**, the slate-built winding house is passed on the left **(7)**. This lies at the top of the former tramway incline down to Glyndyfrdwy station.

Follow the tarmac-surfaced road alongside the winding house, then turn left at the next signposted public footpath. Cross the stile adjacent to the metal farm gate. Follow the right-hand fork in the paths beyond this, commencing where

The Llangollen Railway

the telegraph pole route crosses the footpath **(8)**. This leads steeply down into the woods, crossing another stile in the corner of the field **(9)**. Follow the path back down to the stream alongside the Owain Glyndwr Memorial Hall. Cross the A5 and retrace your steps back downhill to Glyndyfrdwy station.

Walk 8

CARROG

At the road entrance to Carrog station, turn right and follow the B5437 lane towards Carrog village and the river. Cross the stone river bridge **(1)**, then immediately turn right at the T-junction to follow the lane towards Glyndyfrdwy.

After passing the white cottage on your left and the water treatment works

WALK 8 – Carrog to Glyndyfrdwy

Distance: 3.75 miles (6 km)

on the right, cross the stile on the left and follow the footpath as it diagonally climbs across a field **(2)**. At the top of the climb, where the path passes a field boundary, turn immediately left and continue uphill until a stile into the woods is reached.

Cross the stile and follow the path to the uneven roadway, taking the left fork and continuing up the hill through the woods **(3)**. At the top of the climb, pass through a metal farm gate **(4)** and proceed

onwards to a large pond/lake. On the northern side of this water feature, cross the stile adjacent to the wooden signpost **(5)**. Take the right-hand fork (keeping eastwards), following the path over the crest until a stile is reached adjacent to a metal farm gate **(6)**. Cross the stile, following

the widening footpath gently downhill before passing through two metal farm gates **(7)**.

At the end of the track, a dilapidated metal gate and signpost are reached **(8)**. Turn right onto the lane and continue downhill for three-quarters of a mile **(9)** until you reach a T-junction **(10)**. Turn left and follow the lane for another three-quarters of a mile until the river bridge at Glyndyfrdwy is reached. Cross the bridge (SP Glyndyfrdwy (A5)) and continue for a short distance until Glyndyfrdwy station is reached.

Walk 9 — CORWEN — LLANGOLLEN RAILWAY

WALK 9 – Corwen to Caer Drewyn Circular Walk

Distance: 2.5 miles (4km)

Turn right out of Corwen station and head towards Green Lane, keeping the Health Centre on your right and the car park on the left. Upon reaching Green Lane turn right **(1)**, following the road as it skirts around the railway's buffer stops and over the River Dee. The course of the long-closed Vale

of Clwyd Railway from Corwen to Rhyl can be seen on the right as you approach the Corwen Leisure Centre.

Cross the B5437 road and follow the footpath along the front of the Leisure Centre **(2)**. The footpath enters the wooded Corwen Cutting, which is on the course of the Vale of Clwyd Railway. Ignore the path that ascends steeply to your right beside the 'Corwen Cutting' welcome

board **(3)**, but proceed until reaching the metal A-frame barrier. Turn right and follow the lane (SP Caer Drewyn), crossing a stream **(4)** and ignoring turnings to your left and right.

About a quarter of a mile beyond the stream, turn right (SP Caer Drewyn) and pass through a wooden gate **(5)**. Perched on the hill in front of you is Caer Drewyn, one of the best-preserved Iron

Age hill forts in Wales. The first small fort here was a small enclosure built against the natural scarp. Today this is only partly visible as a grass-covered bank. The later, larger hill fort can be traced by a dry-stone wall – its design did not incorporate earthen banks and ditches unlike other local hill forts.

At the next fork in the path, it is possible to explore Caer Drewyn in greater detail and enjoy the vistas from the hill top by taking the left-hand path (SP Caer Drewyn) **(6)**.

However, to proceed with our walk, take the right-hand fork (SP Corwen) and skirt through the bracken along the hillside **(7)**. At the second fork, turn right again (SP Corwen) and proceed through the wooden

Walk 9 Corwen to Caer Drewyn Circular Walk

gate. Descend along the lane **(8)**, then turn right when the B5437 road is reached at a T-junction **(9)**. Go a few paces along the road before carefully crossing outside the Leisure Centre. Retrace your steps along Green Lane to return to Corwen station.

Walk 10

CORWEN

While Corwen is the western terminus of the Llangollen Railway's tracks, it is still possible to explore the route of this long-lost railway line westwards as far as the next village, Cynwyd. This walk predominantly follows the old trackbed of the line and remains close to the River Dee throughout.

Leaving Corwen station, cross the car park and head towards the

WALK 10 – Old railway Circular Walk from Corwen

Distance: 5 miles (8 km)

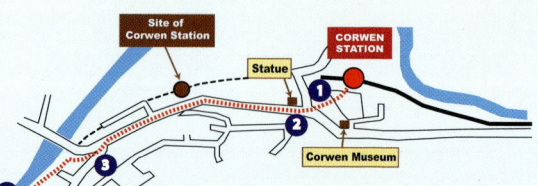

town's square **(1)**. The life-size bronze statue of Owain Glyndwr on his battle horse **(2)** was installed in 2007 and is set on an 8-ton plinth of Welsh granite.

Follow the A5 westwards for half a mile, passing the original Corwen railway station on your right (now an Ifor Williams Trailers showroom). Corwen's original railway goods shed also survives

2

and is passed on the right after the Police & Fire Station.

At the junction of the A5 and B4401 roads, carefully cross the A5 and take the public footpath on your right (SP Brenig Way and North Berwyn Way) **(3)**. This footpath joins the old trackbed adjacent to an infilled former railway bridge under the

3

A5. Proceed for three-quarters of a mile along the footpath **(4-5)** until a wooden gate is reached adjacent to a cottage on your left. A short deviation is possible here to the medieval Llangar Old Parish Church (SP Eglwys Llangar/Llangar Church) **(6)**.

Cross the stile adjacent to a wooden gate **(7)** and continue along the old trackbed for another half a mile. Turn left

Walk 10 Old Railway Circular Walk from Corwen

at the waymarker for the Brenig Way and cross the field until another stile is reached. Pass over the stile and proceed along the gently climbing path until the B4401 road is reached at the top. Turn right and follow the road into the centre of Cynwyd village.

Upon reaching the Prince of Wales public house, turn right (SP Ffatri Ifor Williams Factory) **(8)** and follow the lane down the hill. Care is needed on the

lower section of this in the absence of a pavement.

On top of the old railway bridge, turn right **(9)** and follow the steps down into the wooded cutting (SP Corwen 2 miles). Proceed along the old trackbed **(10)**, retracing your steps until Corwen's new station is reached.

Walk 10 Old Railway Circular Walk from Corwen

Index to locations

Berwyn 24, 25, 30
    Chain bridge 24, 26, 30;
    Hotel 23-24, 26, 31
Bryn Howel Hotel 9
Caer Drewyn Iron Age fort 47-48
Carrog 41
Corwen 45, 50
    Former railway station 50
    Town square 50
Cynwyd 53
Dinas Brân Castle 12-13
Horseshoe Falls and Meter House 27, 29, 31
Glyndyfrdwy 37, 38
    Owen Glyndwr Memorial Hall 37, 40
    Tramway incline 39
Llangar Old Parish Church 52
Llangollen Canal 8, 20, 27
    King's Bridge 26, 31, 35
    Wharf and basin 20-21

Llangollen 6, 10, 14, 20
    Capel Pont Felin Hen Methodist chapel 18
    Centenary Square 19
    International Musical Eisteddfod 22
    Motor Museum 23
    No 18 Church Street 18
    Victoria Promenade 17
Llantysilio 29;
    Hall 31;
    St Tysilio's Church 28
Pandy Mill and Cottage 37-39
Plas Newydd House 16-17;
    Water Tower 17
Sun Bank Halt 9
Trevor station 9
Vale of Clwyd Railway 45-46
Valle Crucis Abbey 35
Velvet Hill 34-35

Further reading

This new edition of the popular Guide Book provides a background history of the railway, followed by a journey along the 10-mile line from station to station. Our journey takes us from Llangollen to Corwen, calling at Berwyn, Glyndyfrdwy and Carrog along the way.

The *Llangollen Railway Visitor Guide* is the ideal companion for a trip along this popular preserved line. The guide also provides the history of the railway's rebirth, the facilities on offer, details of the locomotives and rolling stock that has been used on the line, and much more. This book is sure to prove popular with visitors, would-be visitors and of course railway enthusiasts nationwide.

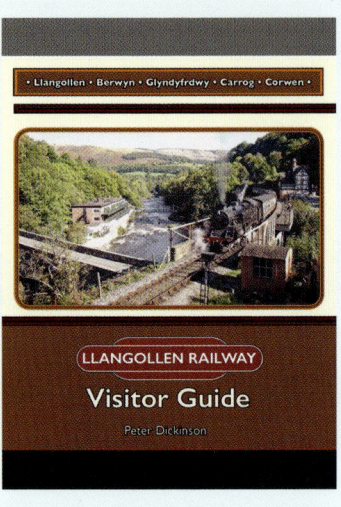

ISBN: 978 1 85794 550 8   £8.99

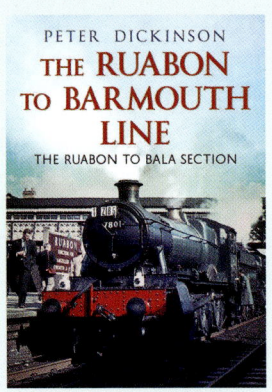

In its heyday, a journey over the Ruabon to Barmouth line was described by the Great Western Railway as 'a country rich in mountain streams, wild woods and wide views, unbeaten in any part of Wales.'

The cross-country Ruabon to Barmouth railway was originally built to fulfil the desire of connecting the town of Llangollen with the rest of the rapidly expanding network. The local Victorian promoters received the backing of the Great Western Railway, which had an ambitious plan to reach the Cambrian coast and tap into the slate quarries around Snowdonia. As time was to prove, the GWR was to be temporarily thwarted by the construction of a branch inland from Barmouth by the rival Cambrian Railways, resulting in an end-on connection between the two railways in the market town of Dolgelly. The route developed into an important artery across rural Wales, bringing in its wake a revolution in agriculture, industry and daily life.

Holiday traffic became big business, tapping into the big conurbations of Liverpool, Manchester and Birmingham. The route would ultimately succumb to the Beeching 'axe' during the 1960s, but even this did not go to plan following severe flooding a few weeks earlier.

Volume 1 of *The Ruabon to Barmouth Line* explores the eastern half of the route, encompassing the towns of Ruabon, Llangollen, Corwen and Bala, and a brief introduction to the fundamentals of railway travel.

ISBN: 978 1 781552 14 8   £18.99